The Haunted House

Story by Joy Cowley • Illustrations by Rodney McRae

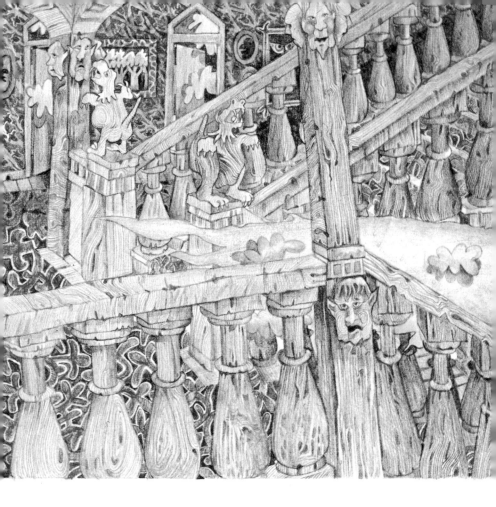

I am a ghostie,
a big, scary ghostie.

2

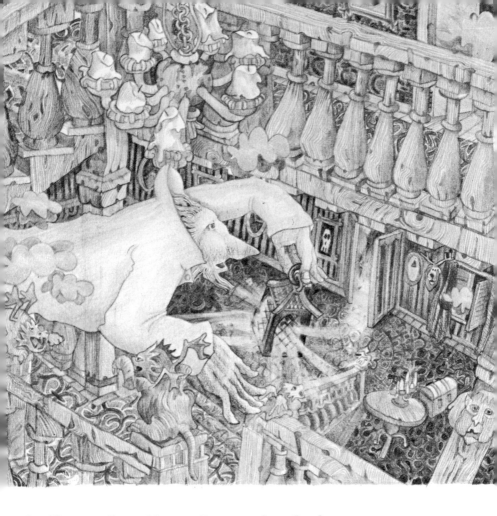

I live in the haunted house,
and I go...

4

00:00.00

I am a spook owl,
a big, scary spook owl.

6

I live in the haunted house,
and I go...

I am a monster,
a big, scary monster.

10

I live in the haunted house,
and I go...

12

I am Antonio,
a little boy, Antonio.

I am in the haunted house,

14

and I'm not scared of **you.**

Shoo! Shoo! Shoo!